AF439987

INTRODUCTION

Find yourself feeling lost in the world of tea? You're not alone. Millions of new tea drinkers find it difficult to navigate the basics. From choosing between different flavors to executing conflicting brewing techniques, it can be overwhelming for people who are new to tea drinking.

That's why we've created a beginner's guide to tea. Here, we'll cover everything from the different tea types and flavor profiles to proper brewing methods using the right teaware. With this guide to tea for beginners, you'll have no problem selecting and brewing the perfect cup of tea for your tastes.

The drinking and blending of herbal tea dates back many centuries all over the world and still continues today. The power of plants have been used for medicinal purposes for as long as history has been documented and the ancient Chinese, ancient Egyptians and Babylonians, Sumerians, Indians, Greeks and Romans have used it due to its popularity and obvious health benefits.

Then, tea makers mingle various ingredients to make novel and unique flavors that turn the tea from calming to invigorating blends. A professional blender takes things a stride further to make the tea blend exclusive to the tea brand.

Some tea retailers even give chances to their clients to make the blend in view of selection of teas, infusions or herbs and spices. Tea blend is a fundamental perspective of a tea business making it more interesting and commercial for a number of purchasers. Blending tea is viewed as a technique with an objective of making the ideal taste, fragrance and appearance for every single purchaser and consumer. However, flavor is the ultimate objective in any blend.

CHAPTER ONE

What is a tea blend?

A tea blend is a combination of teas and/or other ingredients to create new flavours. The ingredient list on a tea blend will be of 2 or more items.

Tea blends can be quite simple but they can also be very unique. Not all tea blends are equal. There are tea blends that feature all-natural, raw ingredients. But, there are tea blends that feature flavourings or essential oils, too.

This is because it is often difficult to get the right flavour just from dried fruit pieces. Flavourings (natural or artificial) are added to enhance the taste and aroma.

Some common tea blends out there are Earl Grey, English Breakfast, Genmaicha and Irish Breakfast.

I've highlighted these teas on my blog before and when doing so I always make sure to mention there are no set recipes or formulas for them. This simply means that one tea company may sell an Earl Grey tea that is very different from another tea company.

The final product comes down to what tea was used in the blend and the ratio of the components.

For example, an earl grey tea is generally a black tea with bergamot oil. If two different tea companies are using the same ingredients, but different ratios, this will greatly affect the flavour profile. That's why some earl grey teas may have stronger notes of bergamot oil than others.

China

Many traditions and folklore say that tea was accidently discovered by the Chinese Emperor Shen Nung in 2737 B.C, when nearby tea leaves from the camellia sinensis plant landed in his pot of hot water in which he drank from…..and the rest is history as they say!

Tea became widespread during the Han Dynasty (206BC – 220AD) as containers for tea had been found in tombs from this era. However, it was under the Tang Dynasty (618AD – 907 AD) that it became more popular and between 760AD – 780AD, a writer called Lu Yu wrote his book devoted entirely to tea – "Cha Jing (The Classic of Tea)", which elevated the status of tea greatly.

By the end of the third century, tea had become China's number one beverage as it was revered by the Chinese for its health benefits attributed to it. As time progressed, tea ceremonies emerged and drinking tea shifted from merely medicinal functions to pleasurable functions. By the eighth century, the Chinese were trading their tea across the globe to Tibet, to the Arab lands and the West, to the Turks, to the nomadic tribes of the Himalayas and along the 'silk road' which stretched from India to Macedonia.

Japan

Around the sixth century, tea was introduced to Japan by Japanese Buddhist monks who had travelled to China to learn and study its culture. Tea drinking then became an important part of Japanese culture as the development of tea ceremonies also emerged there and drinking tea became a social event both outdoors and in private homes.

Portuguese traders and missionaries were probably the first Europeans to try tea and bring back samples, but it was the Dutch who were the first to ship it in bulk to Europe at the beginning of the 17th century. They had developed trade relations with China and had established a trading post on the island of Java. It was via Java, in 1606, that the first shipped distribution of tea from China to Holland was made.

From the outset, tea became a fashionable trend but was only popular amongst the aristocracy and the wealthy due to its high price. This was as a result of their delicate leaves frequently deteriorating on the long sea journeys from China, forcing the profit-conscious Chinese tea producers to adopt more refined methods of manufacturing, packing and transporting.

Russia

The history of tea in Russia can be traced back to around 1618, when tea was offered as gifts by the Chinese to Tzar Michael I (aka Tzar Alexis). By the end of the 17th century, China and Russia engaged in trade relations and after a trade agreement in 1689, tea was regularly imported in exchange for furs, via caravans of hundreds of camels travelling the year-long journey. Thus making tea a precious commodity at the time and establishing alliances between the East and the West.

France

The reputation of drinking tea quickly spread across the continent and by 1636 it had reached France where it enjoyed a brief period of popularity in Paris around 1648.

Britain

Tea was then introduced in Britain around 1660 and the importing of tea began with the marriage of King Charles II to the Portuguese princess Catherine of Braganza. She was a big tea enthusiast and bought her love for the drink to the country and established it as a fashionable beverage amongst the nobility and wealthy. Tea had still remained a luxury partly because of the high taxes imposed on its' import. A pound of tea back then would have cost the average labourer the equivalent of nine months in wages!

Tea instantly became Britain's most important item of trade from China and by 1750, it had become the most popular drink in Britain. With the growth of imports to the West and the development of fast sailing ships like the 'Clippper' (which decreased the time it took to sail from China to Europe), the price of tea consequently dropped, thus becoming popular with the masses. Tea drinking transformed into a social pastime and eventually the 'afternoon tea' became part of British culture.

America

Towards the beginning of the 18th century, the love of tea arrived in America and quickly became a desirable drink. Tea played a crucial role in the American Revolution as the British Empire placed taxes on the tea supply to the colonies of North America who were under their power. This was a major factor in the revolution and the formation of the Boston Tea Party whose struggle for independence marked the beginning of the American War of Independence.

Tea Blending Components

A tea blend usually consists of a tea base, but that base can sometimes also be a dried herb.

Pure teas used in a tea blend can be any type of tea. It's most common to see tea blends that have a black or green tea base, but white, oolong and puerh are also used.

Yellow teas are more rare, therefore it is not common to find that type of tea blended.

Tea blends that feature true tea — from the Camellia Sinensis plant — are caffeinated.

Herbal tea blends start with a base like rooibos, chamomile, peppermint, tulsi, etc. These are naturally caffeine-free and do not come from the tea plant.

However, some herbal tea blends can be caffeinated. Yerba mate and guayusa don't come from the tea plant, so they are technically herbal teas, however, they are caffeinated herbs.

Teas, whether herbal or true, are often blended with other herbs, spices, fruits, roots, flowers and sometimes flavourings.

What makes a good tea blend?
As a traditional tea lover, I have always assumed that a good tea blend doesn't mask the taste of the true tea base.

If I want a green tea based blend, then I don't want it to only taste like the other components added. I want to experience those vegetal or marine notes as well.

But, what's good to me might not be good to someone else as we all have different taste preferences.

When tea blending, it is important to get your base, middle and top notes to all work in perfect harmony.

If the base is weak, the blend will taste thin. If the top notes are overshadowed by a heavy base then you won't have any sparkle.

Tea Blending & Music Correlation

One tea can have a variety of notes and another tea will have those different notes as well. When you put them together you get a beautiful chord that resonates just like in music.

Why do we blend tea?

There are times that you may come across just one pure tea that offers all the flavours that could be from a blend.

This is where tea blending can come in.

With tea blending, you can take two or more teas and combine them. If done well enough, they will fill in the gaps or missing pieces of each other.

Tea Blending Tools

To begin blending tea at home, you need a few tools.

– scale

– tea spoon

– tea and other components/ingredients

– small mixing bowl

– 2-3 equal size cups, white interior (more than 1 is needed as you'll be doing side-by-side tastings)

– tea infuser/filters

– timer

– notebook and writing utensil

A small scale is best for accurate blending and tasting. However, if you do not have a scale, follow the approximate conversions listed below.

1 teaspoon = 2 grams

1/2 teaspoon = 1 grams

1/4 teaspoon = 0.5 grams

How to Make Your Own Tea Blends

It's time to experiment with blending tea at home! Here's what to do:

Decide on a simple blend or complex blend.

Simple tea blends are a bit more straight forward. They consists of 1-3 ingredients and can sometimes just be a blend of pure teas (i.e. Irish Breakfast).

Complex tea blends can consists of 3 or more ingredients and will involve more added flavours (i.e. Lavender Earl Grey Cream).

As a tea blending beginner, I found it easier to start with a simple blend and grow into a complex blend from there. Simple tea blends will often be great as is, but there are times you may want to expand on the flavour profile and add additional ingredients.

Begin with something that you enjoy and know well. If you drink more pure teas, try a simple blend first. If you usually drink flavoured, floral or fruity tea blends, try a complex blend first.

So, once you have selected the components (tea and ingredients) you want to work with follow the other tips below.

Before blending, steep and taste each of the components separately. That includes the tea but also rose petals, cinnamon bark, lavender, dried apple pieces, etc. Basically anything else you want to use in a blend!

This will help you understand the flavour profiles and how they may or may not work together.

Keep the steeping guidelines in mind, too. For example, if you're blending a white and black tea together, they use different water temperatures and steep times. They can blend successfully but consider the appropriate temperature and time to use depending on the ratio.

If you're using dried herbs, be safe and research any side effects or warnings prior to blending.

Weigh the components and make 2 or more blend variations at a time.
When beginning a tea blend, the total weight should equal 2-2.5 grams or roughly 1 teaspoon. This will be enough for you to prepare the tea in one 8 ounce cup/mug for tasting as it's recommended to blend a single serving of tea first. Not only does this make it easier when changes are made to a recipe, less tea is wasted as well.

Weigh the tea and ingredients individually and add them to a small mixing bowl once you reach the total weight. Toss the components together to blend then steep appropriately. I like using a tea cupping set.

Cups or mugs with a white interior is suggested so you can have a better look at the appearance of the infusion.

As mentioned in the list of tools needed for tea blending, more than one cup or mug is needed. This is because you should create 2 or more variations of a blend. Preparing them at the same time is ideal as a side-by-side tasting will help you accurately compare the variations.

The variations don't necessarily have to be very different. In fact, they can be quite similar. Sometimes one blend might just have 0.3 grams less of an ingredient than another. Depending on the component, small changes can make a big difference in taste.

Keep in mind how the final tea blend will be consumed.
After you have all your components set and begin some experiments, think about how the flavours and aromas go together. Ask yourself what's the best way to highlight them?

Would this tea blend shine better without milk?

Is this blend going to be a wellness tea?

Would a sweetener help accentuate the flavours?

Are you looking for a blend that would be best as a tea latte?

Keeping this in mind is important for the end product. For example, if you're making a malty black tea blend that would be best with milk, you may not want to add ingredients like lemon or hibiscus as the acidity in those components can cause milk to curdle.

Another example is if you're looking to create a blend that will promote better sleep you may want to stay away from caffeinated ingredients and focus more on herbs like chamomile or valerian root.

Document everything.
Always bring a notebook and writing utensil to the tea blending station! You need to document ingredients used, measurements, flavour combinations, and experiments.

This is because you may not nail the perfect blend on the first try, maybe not even on the first few tries. That's okay! It's quite common.

In fact, the first few blends I tried myself with the Proper Cuppa Tea Blending Kit were major fails on my part. I had to adjust them a few times as they resulted in either a bitter taste or one flavour overpowered another. Trial and error!

So, the formula or recipe for a tea blend will change frequently. If you write down everything, then you'll have an easier time remembering all the different ingredients, measurements and combinations you tried.

Taste test often and write more notes!
I know I just spoke about documenting everything for the tea blend recipe. But, you can't forget to also actually record all of your tasting notes too!

When you are tasting a tea you should make note of both the aroma and flavour. Even observe the dry and wet leaves. Is the tea blend too strong? Weak? Bitter? Flat? Oily? Tasting notes can be detailed or short and sweet.

Ultimately, you are want to blend a tea that tastes great to you. So, keep making more variations and keep tasting until you have a winner!

Then, you can cross out the formulas or recipes that didn't work for you and your taste buds. Save the perfect one so you can replicate it and make a larger batch!

Popular Tea Blends

Let's look at some of the most common tea blends on the market that we may already be familiar with. By breaking down the ingredients, you can see what goes into the blend.

Earl Grey (Ceylon or Assam tea, bergamot oil, orange peel, cornflowers)

Chai (Assam tea, cinnamon, cardamom, cloves, star anise)

Marrakesh Mint (Gunpowder tea, mint leaves)

English Breakfast (Assam tea, Kenyan tea, Ceylon tea)

Marrakesh Mint Green Tea

There's a formula for every tea blend. The use of true teas (black, green, oolong, yellow, or white,) spices, herbs, fruits, and flavorings can include a multitude of formulas to create a specific blend. The sky's the limit in how creative a blend can get.

Some tea blending formula examples:

True Tea + Another True Tea (English Breakfast)

True Tea + Another True Tea + Spice (Chai)

True Tea + Fruit + Herbs + Flavoring (Earl Grey)

Herbs + Fruit + Spice + Flavoring (Mayan Chocolate Truffle)

Herbs + Fruit (Scarlet Herbal, Pomegranate Berry)

Steps To Blending Your Own Tea

Blending your own tea is a craft and takes time to prepare and carefully claim flavors in teas, spices, fruits, herbs, and flavors before you get all "mad scientist" in your kitchen. We recommend that you invest the time to become acquainted and comfortable in each step before proceeding to the next.

Step #1: Get To Know Your Ingredients

Popular tea blends are the result of many hours of tasting, blending, re-blending, and trying again. "Trial and error" will become your best friend.

We HIGHLY recommend that you indulge your palate with a tea journey to experience and explore various teas before embarking on tea blending. Unless you know what a certain true tea tastes like, it's impossible to effectively pair it with other ingredients.

To begin that tea journey, we have a Tea Journey Starter Set that is perfect for such an occasion!

The ingredients that go into a tea blend must be something you are familiar with in taste, sight, and pairings. Some teas or herbs may not pair well with a fruit or another tea. To help give you an idea of ideal pairings when it comes to tea, herbs, spices, and infusions (flavorings, fruit, etc.,) we have outlined a few below.

Tea Base

This will be the foundation of your tea blend that sets the tone on what type of pairings you will add. Everything should complement one another in flavor. Tea blends are very personal, and what one person likes, another may not.

Tea Base = true teas (black, green, oolong, yellow, or white)

Infusions
Infusions
Infusions are elements that are added to a tea base to flavor it, enhance it, and marry it to any added herbs.

Infusions = dried/fresh fruit/fruit peel, essential oil, artificial flavoring, cacao nibs, chocolate.

Herbs
Herbs are something that requires a bit of exploring because there are various dimensions of flavors in an herb. When tasting one, ask yourself if that particular herb complements the overall tea or fights against it. Dried herbs for tea blends may taste one way out of the jar and yet another once the tea is brewed. It's best to taste the herb in both forms (dried and brewed.)

When it comes to herbs, less is more. Adding too much causes a tea to have a very unpleasant flavor (for example: too much lavender causes a soapy tasting tea.)

Herbs = dried/fresh herbs (leaves, whole plant, plant parts, flowers)

Use Caution With Herbs
Before adding herbs to your tea blends, we recommend that you do your homework on herbs and potential side effects, adverse reactions, and toxicity. This is especially important if you have any medical conditions, are taking medications, are undergoing chemotherapy, or are pregnant or nursing.

So, how do you make an herbal blend that isn't harmful? Unfortunately, we don't have the medical expertise to advise or make recommendations on what herbs to use. This is why we encourage doing a bit of research on herbs before using them.

There are hundreds of herbs that are documented as having potential harmful side effects/adverse reactions. A published research study includes a chart that lists a few herbs.

Spices

Spices are akin to "the frosting on the cake" by giving tea additional layers of flavor. Just as herbs, become well acquainted with how each tastes before adding to a tea.

Spices = dried/fresh

Step #2: Understanding How Blends Coincide With Seasons/Mood

Have you noticed that come fall and wintertime, we tend to gravitate more towards teas that are spicy, nutty, and warming? Our preferences in teas change with seasons and our moods. When tired or depressed, a minty tea is a great pick-me-up. Summer and springtime, we are more prone to indulge in fruity, floral teas.

Fruity Blends

Season: spring, summer

Mood: happy, optimistic

Flavor profile: citrus, berry, melon, apple, pear, sweet, floral

Tea base: Assam, Ceylon, Darjeeling, White, Yellow

Infusion: dried/fresh strawberry, apple, peach, pear, pineapple, orange, lemon, peel, bergamot

Herbs: chamomile, lemon verbena, mint, cornflowers, lemongrass

Spice: sumac

Floral Blends

Season: spring, summer

Mood: melancholy, romantic, content

Flavor profile: floral, sweet, citrus

Tea base: Oolong, White

Infusion: dried/fresh peach, pear

Herbs: jasmine, hibiscus, rose petals, rosehip, cornflowers, elderflower lavender (note: lavender is very strong and does best on its own without anything else added.)

Nutty Blends

Season: fall, winter

Mood: craving, nesting, solitary

Flavor profile: nutty

Tea base: Genmaicha, Dragonwell, Rooibos

Spice: nutmeg

Rooibos Tisane (Herbal Tea)

Spicy Blends

Season: fall, winter

Mood: feisty, craving, festive

Flavor profile: hot, warm

Tea base: Ceylon, Rooibos

Spice: ginger, cloves, anise, cardamom, pepper, nutmeg, cinnamon stick

Sweet Blends

Season: spring, summer

Mood: social, energetic, bright

Flavor profile: malty, honey, melon, fruity, floral

Tea base: Assam, White, Sencha, Oolong, Rooibos

Herbs: chrysanthemum, rosehip, mint, honeybush

Spice: honey

Oolong Tea

Fire Blends

Season: fall, winter

Mood: nesting, solitary, quiet

Flavor profile: cocoa, smoky, toasty, ashy

Tea base: Hojicha, Lapsang Souchong, Ceylon, Raw Pu-erh, Rooibos

Herbs: cacao nibs

Spice: chocolate chips, paprika

Step #3: Gather Appropriate Equipment For Blending

There are a few things you'll need for tea blending—most of which you may already have in your kitchen.

Shot glass (for measuring)

Measuring spoons

Dried spices, fruits, herbs (unless you have access to fresh)

Note: you can dehydrate your own using a dehydrator.

Airtight containers

Base teas: loose-leaf true tea (such as Assam, Ceylon, Rooibos, etc.)

Flavoring

Step #4: Begin Your Blending

NOW it's time to become that mad scientist we mentioned earlier. You can start with three of your favorite herbs. Experiment with combinations of true tea, herbs, fruits, spices, and flavorings and create something you can call your own. If you would rather play it safe and save time, there are a ton of tea blending recipes online.

Step #5: Store Your Blend Properly

It's important to store your newly blended tea in an airtight container while being careful not to include any moist/wet/damp particles or items in with the tea.

Sometimes if fresh herbs or fruits are used in a blend, it can cause the tea to become damp, which leads to mold. Adding fresh herbs directly to your hot tea creates a bright flavor finish.

Blending Bliss Is At Your Fingertips

So, now you don't have to wonder, "How do you make your own tea blends?" You'll get the process perfected and may even find that you'll come up with new creations that will tantalize your palate!

Tea leaves can be flavoured in many ways in making of the making of a blend.

Inclusions: the direct addition of fruits, blossoms, herbs or other additives to tea leaves for the visual and/or sensory effect.

Extracts: are flavoring agents derived by extracting the essential oils from the leaves, fruits, blossoms, roots or other parts of a plant. Extracts carry the distinctive scents or flavors that we come to expect from that plant.

Natural Identical (NIs): flavoring agents that are obtained with the aid of chemical synthesis by a chemist. NIs tend to be more stable than extracts and are usually significantly less expensive. Many flavored products are flavored with nature-identical flavors.

Artificial Flavors are created by altering the chemical structure of a naturally occurring molecule to create a different & more intense compound.

Scenting derive their flavor simply from physical proximity to strong flavors. While some jasmine teas may be artificially flavored, "real" jasmine teas are scented with Jasmine blossoms which are then removed (jasmine blossoms have a much shorter shelf life than tea). Lapsang Souchong is scented by being exposed to the smoke of burning pine root.

Very often, these method are Combined to create our flavoured tea blends as most inclusions alter the flavor of the cup but are usually not strong enough to deliver the punch we want. Hence most "flavored" teas, are further combined with NIs. The total amount of flavouring applied depends on the flavor and desired strength, but usually falls between 0.5% - 5% of the weight of the tea being flavored.

The flavouring agent is poured or sprayed over the dry leaf subsequently mixed to ensure an even distribution. Larger companies do this in large rotating drums filled with hundreds of kilograms of tea. Most teas can be flavored (properly absorbing the extract) in under 30 minutes, though some flavors do require significantly longer.

Principles In Tea Blending

The following will be the 3 key ingredients in creating a beautiful tea blend :

Objectives - What are we making the tea blend for? Would we want to create a wellness cocktail for the health benefits of the additives we use or simply for the gourmet & artisanal factor of creating a exquisitely crafted tea blend that brews well in a cup?

Secondly, from a technical standpoint, tea blending is about balance.

Aesthetically beautiful dried leaves

Rounded & balance bouquet or aroma [more applicable with extracts & NIs

Taste & structure of the mouth-feel

Finish

Last but not least, the most important factor in creating a tea blend is the intrinsic factor of emotions. Tea blending can be an exercise of empathy where tea leaves & herbs, when put together, are used to invoke a feeling or to tell a story of my own.

Summary of Tea Blending Ingredients

BLENDING INGREDIENT	TASTE	MAINLY USED AS	NOTES
Bamboo Leaves	Smooth, full bodied with herbaceous taste	Herbal Infusion or addition to a herbal blend	Great interesting leaf shape and colour. Similar to green tea and has full bodied taste - try blending with more neutral taste ingredients such as Sweet Orange Peel or Cornflower Petals for a truly great tasting, vibrant blend.
Calendula Petals	Neutral	Visual Decoration	Fantastic, vibrant colour that will add

			interest to any blend.
Chrysanthemu m Flowers	Floral, with long lingering finish	Herbal Infusion or addition to a herbal blend	Try pairing with a green tea such as Long Jing.
Clanwilliam Rooibos	Fruity with sweet notes	Herbal Infusion or addition to a herbal blend	Really versatile herb used as a base for many herbal tea blends.
Cornflower Petals	Neutral	Visual Decoration	When infused alone creates a slightly blue infusion.
Dried Ginger Root	Excellent clean taste with hot ginger finish	Herbal Infusion or addition to a herbal blend	Great blending ingredient that will add a warmth to any tea or herbal blend.
Egyptian Camomile	Fruity with a light floral flavour	Herbal Infusion or addition to	Apple-like flavour adds a layer of

		a herbal blend	depth to any herbal blend. Try adding Orange Peel or Spearmint.
Green Yerba Mate	Vegetative green leaves	Herbal Infusion or addition to a herbal blend	Contains both high levels of caffeine and antioxidants. Blends well with Peppermint or Spearmint.
Hibiscus Flowers	Sweet, honey-like tangy taste, similar to pomegranate or lemonade	Herbal Infusion or addition to a herbal blend	Popular with the stars like Beyonce! Very versatile blending ingredient which when infused will add a deep, bright burgundy red colour to the infusion.

Honeybush	Refreshing and cleansing with hints of honey	Herbal Infusion or addition to a herbal blend	High in antioxidants, a great blending ingredient to add both interest and taste to a blend.
Jasmine Petal & Flowers	Very mild, tending neutral	Visual Decoration	Will blend well with most teas - particularly as a colour accent.
Lavender De Provence	Slightly pungent, distinctive flavour	Layer of taste in a blend and visual decoration	Versatile blending component that can complement most types of teas. Can be overpowering if used too much, so add in stages and test blend profile regularly.
Lemon Balm	Herbaceous lemon	Layer of taste in a	Works well when added

	notes, slightly dry cup	blend and visual decoration	to green tea like Japan Sencha. Try ratio 1 part Sencha to ¼ part Lemon Balm.
Lemon Verbena	Slightly dry with hints of sweet lemon	Layer of taste in a blend and visual decoration	Try blending with a black tea to create a 'lemon' tea.
Lemongrass	Sweet, lemon taste without the normal lemon tang	Used for its sweet lemon taste but without the tangy flavour normally experienced with lemon.	Very popular and versatile blending ingredient for taste but also gives a great visual impact too.
Lime Leaves	Strong and sweet citrus notes	Layer of taste in a blend and visual decoration	Particularly good with black tea blends and Lemongrass.
Linden Flowers	Sweet & Fruity with	Herbal Infusion or addition to	Try blending with other herbal

	a smooth finish	a herbal blend	infusions such as Rooibos, Camomile Lemon Verbena.
Liquorice Root Pieces	Sweet with anise like character	Herbal Infusion or addition to a herbal blend	Contains up to 14% naturally occurring sugars so has a naturally sweet character. Blends especially well with Egyptian Camomile and Peppermint.
Mate Green Egyptian Lemon	Slightly sweet with palate cleansing Egyptian lemon.	Herbal Infusion or addition to a herbal blend	Contains Mateine, a derivative of caffeine. Blends well with green tea and other herbals.

Nettle Leaves	Dry with a herbaceous finish.	Herbal Infusion or addition to a herbal blend	Try blending with other herbal infusions such as Yerba Green Mate, Lemongrass, Peppermint or Spearmint.
Peppermint	Pungent, cool fresh, menthol taste	Herbal Infusion or addition to a herbal blend	Distinctive mint taste will add a refreshing layer to any tea or herbal blend.
Pomegranate Peel	Refreshing, fruity taste, with a hint of zesty lemon	Layer of taste in a blend and visual decoration	Great blending ingredient for use with most teas.
Rose Hip	Mild and fruity with a slight tangy taste.	Herbal Infusion or addition to a herbal blend	Packed with Vitamin C, Rosehips are commonly used as a base for herb

			and fruit infusions.
Spearmint	Cool mint and fresh	Herbal Infusion or addition to a herbal blend	Blend with a Green Gunpowder tea and create your own Moroccan Mint Green tea.
Sunflower Petals	Neutral with a light, slightly musty finish	Visual Decoration	Wonderful vibrant colour to add accent and interest. Will also provide a mild mellow flavour. Try with all types of teas and herbs.
Sweet Orange Peel	Very mild, almost neutral character but with slightly tart, citric notes	Mainly Visual Decoration & Texture	Use sparingly if adding to a tea blend that might be taken with milk - too much orange

			peel will cause milk to curdle.
Tuscany Rosebuds & Petals	A pleasant lingering finish enhanced with light floral notes	Mainly Visual Decoration & Texture	Wonderful colour and light floral flavour that will add interest to most tea blends.
Wild Rosebuds	Pleasant and soothing with soft rose character	Herbal Infusion or addition to a herbal blend	Visually very appealing and offers any blend a definite rose character.

Reasons To Try Blending teas

Blending teas is fascinating and yields appealing flavours and fragrances. This is not only the reason to make the tea blends, there are five reasons you should try making your own blend.

Ensure Consistency In Quality Of Tea Batch

Blending tea is a method for guaranteeing the uniformity in the quality of tea on a large scale. Tea blends should be similar every time and tea producers need to guarantee that each tea mixture possesses the same quality again and again. This is why you generally get prime quality, reliable and astonishing tea blends with regards to commercial teas.

Tea blend is a method of acquiring the health perspectives with an art of drinking and making blends. Tea makers don't believe in making blends with two teas only, they incorporate spices and flavors which possess powerful therapeutic properties. This is the reason tea blends have picked up the steam in China and India. In India, Ayurvedic medicine has been founded on blending herbs and spices and flavor teas for thousands of years. In many parts of the word, Tea blends are used for treatment for a variety of diseases and as a holistic health approach.

Perfect Way To Commercialize Tea

Tea blend is, obviously, a method of advertising the tea. Blending involves inspiring flavors and fragrances, it is a well known method of introducing the amazing tea to each family. Tea retailers and agents trust greatly on tea blends as it guarantees their quality and interest for tea blends remains consistent for their clients.

Give Amazing Flavor And Aroma

Tea blend is a perfect way to enjoy the characteristics of various teas and herbs and spices in a single cup of tea. Various ingredients when combined in a single blend give a unique and astonishing flavor and aroma. It is said that the ultimate objective of a tea blend is to get an appealing flavor and fragrance.

Turn Non-Tea Buyers To clients

Tea blend yields a characteristic flavor and taste offering a huge variety of health benefits. It is additionally an astounding method for getting non-tea buyers to become keen on tea, which brings about new clients.

Ways To Create Your own Tea Blends

Blending is not a new idea, blending tea with herbs and spices has been used for thousands of years. Blending tea has gained popularity in recent years as the advanced tea customers generally look for new and fascinating tea blends with a characteristic taste and aroma. This is the reason blending procedures are advancing continually. There are various exciting ways tea dealers mix and join teas.

Mixing Herbs

The most popular blending procedure is to incorporate different types of herbs and spices. Most commonly used herbs and spices for blending teas are peppermint, hibiscus, spearmint, chamomile, rose and ginger. These herbs and spices are blended in various quantities to yield a new and interesting flavor. These herbal tea blends are incorporated with various herbs and spices like turmeric, cinnamon, dried fruits and other herbs for different flavor and aroma.

Herbs are mixed with an aim of special flavor and fragrance or due to their therapeutic properties. In some cases, the actual tea is forgotten and the blend comprises only herbs and spices. The justification behind is the requirement of making decaffeinated tea, obviously a simple herbal tea.

As far as the blending process is concerned, it can be carried out by hand as small tea sellers do, or it may also be done in blending drums for business purposes at large scales. Consistency of blend, weight and percentage of all the ingredients are noticed carefully. Consistent quality of each batch of tea blend is significant to keep the clients faithful to your brand.

Ingredients

Ingredients are usually added that give tea blend an artistic value and possess beneficial health effects. These ingredients don't influence the flavor and fragrance of the blend, instead they only change the chemical composition and health effects of the blend. These inclusions do not add to the flavor profile, however, they definitely change the color and visual incitement for you.

Essence

Usually tea gets its aroma from the surrounding area where it is grown, fermented and dried. However, essence is also used to give the tea a specific aroma, for instance bergamot oil is used to scent black tea and jasmine is added to green and white tea.

Moreover, essential oils are also used to add essence to the tea. These oils are sprinkled on tea leaves batches that guarantee equal distribution of essence.

Process To Create Your Own Blend

To make your own blend at home, you need to add five tbsp. of base tea in a tin. Now add your principal ingredient which may be a tea or herb and spice.

Now, you can add 1 teaspoon of additional spices to the base tea and main ingredient. Try to add fruity or floral flavors which will avoid the disruption of flavor.

These inclusions won't change the flavor of the blend but only add the color, change chemical composition and enhance medical benefits.

Now, essence should be added to the blending tea, you can add a few drops of essential oil to give your blend a unique aroma.

The last step is to place the blend in an airtight container and place it in a cool and dry place for 48 hours or more time.

CHAPTER TWO

DIY Recipes for Your Own Tea Blends

Rose Breakfast Blend

Breakfast blends are usually a mix of stronger and lighter teas in the ratio that gives a recognizable breakfast tea flavor. The most common teas in breakfast blends come from India and Sri Lanka, although teas from other countries are now used as well. For the traditional Breakfast Blend, use Darjeeling and Assam tea. This tea is perfect with milk.

Ingredients:

2 teaspoons of Darjeeling tea (Namring Estate Darjeeling)

3 teaspoons of Assam tea (Organic Assam)

½ – 1 teaspoon of rose buds

Extra tip: Add guarana powder for an extra caffeine boost.

Tropical Pu'erh

If you want to drink pu'erh because of the benefits but don't quite enjoy the pure flavor, you can easily create your own blend with the flavor that you like the most. Our recommendation is coconut pu'erh because it blends well with the earthly flavor of ripe pu'erh. Adjust the ratio to suit your taste. You can exclude candied fruit and add coconut only.

Ingredients:

2 spoons of Pu'erh tea

1 teaspoon of candied pineapple

1 teaspoon of candied mango

1 teaspoon of shredded coconut

Fast blending: Blend pu'erh tea with your favorite fruit tea.

White Spice tea

Light flavor of white tea blends well with tangy and spicy notes. Peppercorns are a great choice for adding a spicy note and dried strawberries give a tangy and sweet layer to light and delicate flavor of Bai Mu Dan. This tea contains caffeine.

Ingredients:

2 spoons of Pai Mu Tan

½ teaspoon of peppercorns

1 teaspoon of dried strawberries

A pinch of safflower

Extra tip: Do not use flavors and herbs with a strong taste for blending with white tea.

Apple Pie Herbal tea

Sunday dessert in a liquified form? Yes, please. Apple Pie herbal blend has rooibos as a base because of its natural sweet flavor. Besides, this dessert should be suitable for children as well, so we wanted to leave out teas with caffeine. It's easy to blend and makes a cup of tea with a delightful sweet and lightly tangy taste.

Ingredients:

2 spoons of Rooibos tea

1-2 teaspoon of dried apple

1 inch of cinnamon stick

½ inch of vanilla pod

Extra tip: Add white chocolate drops for a creamier and sweeter tea.

Minty Sencha

This minty blend is great both hot and cold, but for the ultimate summer refreshment use cold brewing technique to make an iced tea. For an extra kick add some dried spearmint leaves.

Ingredients:

1 teaspoon dried lemongrass

1 teaspoon of dried mint

2 spoons of Chinese Sencha Green

Extra tip: Add fresh cucumber to the jug or teapot when cold-brewing. Chinese sencha is better choice for blending than Japanese sencha.

Chamomile Herbal

If you are looking for a calming tea without a caffeine that you can drink in the evening, chamomile is the best herb to use. All the herbs in this blend offer calming and soothing properties, especially for the stomach problems. This blend is best hot.

Ingredients:

2 spoons of dried chamomile

½ teaspoon of dried licorice root

1 teaspoon of dried ginger root

Extra tip: For a more potent sleepy time tea replace ginger with valerian root.

Refreshing Hibiscus

Crimson color and refreshing tangy and fresh taste make this herbal blend one of the best summer drinks you can blend yourself. It's great both hot and cold.

Ingredients

2 spoons dried hibiscus

1 teaspoon of mint leaves

1 teaspoon of lemongrass

Extra tip: This tea is great both hot and cold.

Upgraded Earl Grey

Earl Grey, the classical blend beloved by many tea drinkers, you can easily upgrade by adding a pinch of lavender flowers or rose petals. Be careful not to use too much flowers as they will ruin the taste. Both lavender and rose petals have a dominant scent and flavor and should be used in small amounts to add just an extra layer to your blend.

Ingredients

2 teaspoons of regular Earl Grey tea (or feel free to use one of the nontraditional blends and enhance them with more ingredients)

A pinch of Lavender or rose petals

Extra tip: Add safflower for an extra note.

Homemade Chai

The beauty of chai tea is that you can customize your recipe until you get the flavor you truly enjoy. Chai is always made with a black tea base, preferably with stronger Assam tea, milk and a blend of different spices. Crush the spices in a mortar and blend with black tea.

Ingredients:

3-5 spoons of Assam black tea

1 teaspoon of dried ginger

½ teaspoon of peppercorns

2 inches of cinnamon stick

1 teaspoon of cardamom

1 teaspoon of cloves

Extra tip: Add star anise, nutmeg, cocoa shells or vanilla to your blend. Adjust the ratio of spices to black tea leaves to create lighter or stronger taste.

Herbal Chocolate

Liquid chocolate in the healthiest way will satisfy your chocolate needs, especially during rainy cool days. Use boiling water to brew Herbal Chocolate tea to melt the chocolate drops.

Ingredients:

1 teaspoon of chocolate drops

2 spoons of pure Rooibos tea

½ – 1 inch of vanilla pod

½ teaspoons of cocoa shells

Extra tip: Turn this blend to an After Eight tea by adding a pinch of dried mint leaves. Replace rooibos with Yunnan Black tea if you want a stronger flavor and tea with caffeine. Make it in a latte style for extra creaminess.

Herbal Tea blending Recipes

Southern Sipper

1 part spearmint

1 part black tea

Orange zest to taste

Medicinal Properties – Spearmint is a widely used homemade herbal medication. Herbal medicine practitioners have customarily used a tea prepared with the leaves of spearmint to treat medical conditions, such as headaches, fevers, and digestive problems. Black tea has caffeine and as such may be bothersome to some who are not accustomed to drinking caffeinated beverages.

Lemon Up

1 part lemon balm

1 part lemon verbena

½ part lemon thyme

⅛ part lemon zest

Medicinal Properties – Lemon verbena has a number of therapeutic uses. For instance, a placid sedative tea is prepared using the leaves of the herb to comfort nasal and bronchial congestion. In addition, this herbal tea is also taken internally to treat palpitations, indigestion, stomach cramps, flatulence, and nausea. Lemon balm: Traditionally, decoctions made from the lemon balm have always been used to lift up the spirits and perk up morale. The herb is believed to induce longevity when it is taken on a regular basis. There are also many other traditional uses of the herb, such as in the healing of wounds to bring relief from palpitations, relax the heart, and treat toothaches and other dental problems.

M'Lady's Cup

1 part chamomile

1 part red raspberry leaf

½ part peppermint or spearmint (see Southern Slipper)

Just a pinch lavender

Medicinal Properties – Chamomile has a great relaxant action on the nervous system and the digestive system. The herbal remedies made from this herb are considered to be a perfect remedy for the treatment of disorders affecting babies and children. Red raspberry leaf: The raspberry plant is used for its astringent and for its stimulant properties. When a strong infusion or tea of the plant is taken as a mouthwash or as a gargle, it soothes a sore mouth and also lessens inflammation of the mucous membrane of the throat.

Anise Mint

1 part anise hyssop

3 parts spearmint (see Southern Slipper)

Medicinal Properties – Anise hyssop in folk herbal medicine tea has been employed to facilitate the digestive process. Native Americans also used anise hyssop as a medication to cure wounds, fevers, diarrhea, and cough. The leaves of anise hyssop are cardiac (good for the heart) as well as diaphoretic (induces perspiration). An infusion prepared from anise hyssop leaves is used to cure feeble heart and other health conditions. A poultice prepared with the leaves and stems of anise hyssop may be used to heal burn injuries.

Stomach Soother

2 cups of water

2 teaspoons peppermint leaf

½ teaspoon fennel seeds

Pinch of dried ginger

Medicinal Properties – Fennel Seeds Patients affected by abdominal bloating are the main beneficiaries of herbal remedies made from the seeds of the fennel. In addition, the fennel seeds are also used to alleviate problems such as stomach pain; they are used in stimulating poor appetite in patients; the diuretic action and the anti-inflammatory properties of the seeds are also used to treat a variety of disorders affecting different individuals. This tea is delicious, very calming, and great for digestive problems.

Elderberry Tea

2 cups of water

2 tablespoons elderberry syrup (or one heaping tablespoon dried berries)

1 cinnamon stick

2 cardamom pods

Simmer for 30 minutes.

Medicinal Properties – Elderberry: A variety of herbal medications are derived from different parts of the elder plant. For example, the mucous lining of the inner nose and throat is toned by a remedy made from the flowering tops of the plant. This treatment leads to a better resistance from infection in these areas of the body. This tea is helpful when you have a cold or flu.

Love Tea

¾ cup rose petals

¼ cup lavender blossoms

½ cup rosemary

¾ cup jasmine blossoms

½ cup hibiscus flowers

Mix all dried ingredients and store in an airtight container. To make the tea, use 1 teaspoon of the blend for each cup of briskly boiling water. Allow it to steep for 10 minutes. This blend makes a great gift in decorative bottles along with a fancy note about the folklore below!

Folklore: Rose petals to bring or send love. Lavender blossoms indicate devotion.

Rosemary is for remembrance. Jasmine indicates sensuality. Hibiscus flowers: when used behind the left ear, "I have a lover," and behind the right ear, "I want a lover."

Holy Basil-Sage Tea

Scant ¼ cup of dried holy basil leaves

Pinch of dried sweet annie (Artemisia annua) leaves (optional)

Pinch of green tea (I suggest ½ teaspoon)

Two dried sage leaves (I suggest ¼ teaspoon dried powdered sage)

Medicinal Properties – Holy basil has numerous benefits. The leaves of this herb serve as a nerve tonic (stimulate the nerves) and help sharpen memory. The plants also help get rid of phlegm and catarrhal substances accumulated in the bronchial tubes. The leaves of holy basil help make the stomach stronger and bring about profuse sweating. Even the seeds possess medicinal properties, and they secrete mucilage (mucilaginous). In fact, this herb is excellent for diminishing anxiety, stress, and depression.

Rosemary-Mint Tea

Two (4 inch) sprigs rosemary or 2 teaspoons dried

About ¼ cup dried mint, either peppermint or spearmint

Pinch green tea (optional)

Medicinal Properties – Rosemary can circulate blood to the head, thereby aiding in better concentration and improving memory. It is also believed that rosemary helps in better hair growth because it is able to improve blood circulation to the scalp. The versatile herb has even been used to treat varied disorders like vertigo and epilepsy.

American Cranberry Tea

1 quart cranberries

4 quarts water

2½ cups sugar (I recommend substituting ½ cup raw honey)

½ cup cinnamon candies (I recommend substituting 2–3 teaspoons Ceylon cinnamon)

½ teaspoon nutmeg

½ teaspoon cinnamon

½ teaspoon allspice

Juice of 3 oranges

Juice of 3 lemons

Bring cranberries and one quart of water to a boil. In another pan, bring three quarts of water and sugar (or honey) to a boil. Add cinnamon candies (or Ceylon cinnamon), cloves, and spices, then simmer. Put cranberries through a sieve and combine with other liquid. Before serving, add juice of oranges and lemons. Serves 12–15. Sounds like a great Christmas treat.

Medicinal Properties – Cranberries: In the 1840s, German researchers found out that the urine of individuals who consumed cranberries contains hippuric acid, a chemical that combats bacteria. Studies undertaken in recent times endorse the theory that consuming cranberries or drinking the juice of these berries may help in avoiding or combating urinary tract infections. In effect, hippuric acid thwarts the bacterium Escherichia coli (E. coli) from sticking to the lining of the urinary tract.

Memory Tea

Equal parts:

Rose (petals)

Rosemary (see Rosemary-Mint Tea)

Licorice Root

Medicinal Properties – Rose petals: Like rose hips, the petals of rose flowers also have numerous remedial uses. For instance, rose petals are effective in relieving congestion in the female reproductive system. Licorice root: Ancient records from Greece and other places show it was used in the treatment of asthma, chest problems, and canker sores. Licorice is also found to be useful to ease certain chest complaints, arthritis, and inflammation of joints, skin, and eyes.

Garden Tea

Equal parts:

Purple sage leaves

Lemon balm (see Lemon Up)

Peppermint or spearmint

Rose petals (see Memory Tea)

Medicinal Properties – Sage leaves can be used for all types of sore throats. This is because sage has antiseptic and astringents as well as certain relaxing properties, which is one of the main reasons why sage is used rather frequently in gargles. Sage is often described as a digestive tonic and as a stimulant, and in Chinese medicine sage enjoys a good reputation as a versatile nerve tonic.

Seventh Heaven Tea

Equal parts:

Chamomile (see M'Lady's Cup)

Lemon verbena (see Lemon Up)

Lavender Mint Tea
1 part lavender

4 parts peppermint (or spearmint if you like a milder mint)

Medicinal Properties – Lavender is often combined in mixed remedies with different sedative herbs to treat problems such as sleeplessness, nervous irritability, and chronic headaches, as well as persistent migraine problems in affected individuals. The herbal remedy made from the lavender is also very useful in alleviating depression and related mental disorders.

Chamomile-Peppermint Tea
1 part chamomile (see M'Lady's Cup)

1 part calendula

¼ part lemon peel

1 part peppermint

Pinch clove

Medicinal Properties – Calendula: The calendula is a potent antiseptic herb. Several of the active chemical constituents found in the herb are fungicidal or mycotic toxins, especially the resins. In addition, these compounds are also bactericidal and antiviral agents. This accounts for the effectiveness of the herb in the treatment of cuts, physical wounds, varicose veins, and various other inflammatory disorders that affect the human body.

1 part chamomile (see M'Lady's Cup

¼ part lemon peel

1 part peppermint

1 part sage (see Garden Tea)

Pinch clove

Tibetan Butter Tea

This is no ordinary tea. In fact, many tea drinkers don't like it at all because it's not sweet tea but rather creamy and salty. I was a bit confused when I first drank it, thinking it was a broth rather than tea. But I immediately loved it. Tibetan tea, if you can get it, comes in blocks of about a pound or so, with large leaves. It's often wrapped in yellow tissue paper, or you can just use loose-leaf tea (preferably strong black leaf), or even a few tea bags if you have nothing else. Please, do try this tea, especially on a cold day. It's heaven, and it's actually one of my favorite teas now.

2 well-rounded teaspoons of strong, loose black tea, or 3 teabags (if using pressed tea, cut off a chunk about double the size of a quarter)

2 tablespoons salted organic butter (preferably raw or cultured)

Milk (I recommend organic, raw whole milk)

Pinch sea salt

Hand mixer (that can be immersed in fluid)

Boil water in kettle. Place leaves at the bottom of a glass

Add 4 cups boiling water over leaves. Let sit, covered, 3–5 minutes.

Strain leaves. Set aside, then pour back into the pitcher.

Add pinch sea salt and 2 rounded tablespoons organic butter to the tea.

Pour about 2–3 cups whole, raw organic milk, enough to fill pitcher about ⅔ full while still making sure liquid remains hot.

Take hand blender and submerge it into the tea. Mix for a few seconds to make sure butter and salt are properly dispersed. Little oil bubbles will appear on the top of the tea, and it will become light brown. Leave tea in the pitcher if there's a bunch of you, or quickly pour into a teapot with a cozy to keep it warm longer.

Herbal Masala Tea (Chai)

4 cups water

1 tablespoon fresh ginger, peeled and sliced into 4 thin rounds (about 1-inch thick)

4 sticks cinnamon bark, dried

10 whole cloves, dried

10 whole green cardamom pods

10 whole allspice berries

10 whole (black or green) peppercorns

Bring water to a rolling boil in a large pot, about 8 minutes. Add all spices and continue to boil for another 6–8 minutes. Remove from heat. Allow to steep for another 1–2 minutes. Strain to remove whole herbs and spices. Pour into a tea pot or other heatproof container, and serve in cups with cream or milk and honey to taste.

8 cups water

2 whole cinnamon sticks (3-inch pieces)

10 whole cloves

5 green cardamom pods

½ tablespoon fresh orange zest (about 1 small orange)

½ large, whole vanilla beans, split open and scooped out with a knife or spoon to remove essence

1 tablespoon cut licorice root

½ tablespoon anise seeds

1 tablespoon whole Chinese star anise

1 teaspoon cut sarsaparilla (optional)

Bring water to a rolling boil in a large pot, about 8 minutes. Add all spices. Continue to boil for another 6–8 minutes. Remove from heat. Allow to steep for another 1–2 minutes, then strain to remove whole herbs and spices. Pour into a teapot or other heatproof pitcher or container. To serve, pour into tea cups. Tea can be served either hot or as an herbal iced tea.

Masala Chai with Fennel

1 cup water

1 cup organic raw whole milk

3 teaspoons Assam, Ceylon, or Darjeeling tea leaves (if these teas are not readily available, I recommend black tea)

1-inch piece dry ginger

3 cardamom pods, split open

2 peppercorns

2 whole cloves

1-ince piece cinnamon

1 teaspoon fennel seeds

Sugar to taste (I recommend raw honey)

Coarsely grind all spices together and set aside. Mix milk and water in a saucepan. Bring to a boil on high. As the milk/water rises to a boil, add the spice mix. Reduce to a simmer. When it rises to a boil again, add the tea leaves. Allow to rise, then turn off heat. Cover and steep for 2 minutes. Strain, add sugar, and enjoy.

Green Tea Chai

2 tablespoons green tea leaves (I use powdered green tea)

6 whole cloves

½ teaspoon ground ginger

¼ teaspoon ground cloves

1 teaspoon ground Ceylon cinnamon

1 cup organic raw milk

4 cups filtered water

Honey to taste

Boil water, then simmer with Ceylon cinnamon, ginger, and cloves for about 10 minutes. Add tea and steep 5 minutes. Add milk and heat to near boiling. Turn off heat. Strain out spices and tea leaves. Serve with honey.

Medicinal Properties – Green Tea: As an herbal measure, green tea is helpful in the treatment of various infections affecting the digestive tract of patients. It is believed to induce sweating and is used as a tonic for frayed nerves. Green tea is also used for the treatment of various eye problems. It is used in the treatment of hemorrhoids, to treat physical tiredness and fatigue, and to bring down fever in patients. The leaves of the tea plant can also be used as a topical herbal measure for the external treatment sunburn.

Orange Spiced Black Tea

This tea blend was inspired by the fancy tea blend I bought in southern France. At first I made a similar blend without the orange extract but the orange taste was never strong enough. Then I got the idea of adding the extract and finally the orange flavor popped out. As a result, the dried oranges in this blend are more about their beautiful appearance than actual taste.

To dry your own oranges, slice an orange into thin segments, lay them on a glass baking sheet and dry them on low in the oven. Turn them over every once in awhile. Once they are completely dried, cut them into triangle wedges as seen in the photo.

What you'll need

1 teaspoon orange extract

1 cup Assam tea (or black tea of your choice)

1 tablespoon rainbow peppercorns

Handful of dried orange slices

1 tablespoon cinnamon chips

1 tablespoon cardamom pods, slightly crushed

Need organic herbs or supplies?

Get them here!

This post is sponsored by our friends at Mountain Rose Herbs.

Place the teaspoon of orange extract into a quart glass jar. Shake well to distribute the liquid all over the jar.

Add the assam tea, pepper, orange slices, cinnamon and cardamom. Shake really well.

Let this sit for a day or two to allow the extract to soak in to the tea and spices.

To brew: Use 1 heaping teaspoon per 8 ounces of hot water. Steep for 3 to 5 minutes. Strain and enjoy as is or with milk, cream, honey or sugar.

Vanilla Earl Grey with Cornflowers

This is one of my favorite tea blend recipes. I am admittedly very smitten with Earl Grey tea these days. This blend adds a vanilla flavor as well as some beautiful blue flowers to brighten up the mix.

What you'll need

1 cup Earl Grey tea

2 tablespoons cornflowers (Centaurea cyanus)

1 vanilla bean, chopped finely

Combine all the ingredients together.

To brew: Use 1 heaping teaspoon per 8 ounces of hot water. Steep for 3 to 5 minutes. Strain and enjoy as is or with milk, cream, honey or sugar.

Forest Tea Blend

I was inspired to make this blend using Mountain Rose Herbs' Ancient Forest Tea, which is grown "exclusively from stands of protected ancient growth tea plants in the Yunnan province of China, all of which range in age from 500 to 2,700 years old."

To this I've added the resinous western redcedar leaves and the aromatic hawthorn leaves and flowers, making this a delicious forest blend.

What you'll need

1 part Ancient Forest tea

1 part western redcedar (Thuja plicata)

1/2 part hawthorn leaves (Crataegus spp.)

Process the western redcedar leaves into small pieces. Combine all the ingredients together.

To brew: Use 1 heaping teaspoon per 8 ounces of hot water. Steep for 3 to 5 minutes. Strain and enjoy as is or with milk, cream, honey or sugar.

Smokey Pu'erh Tea

Pu'erh tea is a popular fermented tea that is highly prized by tea connoisseurs. This blend combines the fermented tea of pu'erh with the smoky taste of lapsang souchong tea. The chrysanthemum flowers taste good as well but are mainly added for appearance in this blend.

3 parts pu'erh tea

2 parts chrysanthemum flowers

1 part lapsang souchong tea

Combine all the ingredients together.

To brew: Use 1 heaping teaspoon per 8 ounces of hot water. Steep for 3 to 5 minutes. Strain and enjoy as is or with milk, cream, honey or sugar.

Herbal Digestive Blend

This is a delicious tea that can be used to support healthy digestion or simply enjoyed for the taste. Licorice root may cause high blood pressure when taken in large amounts frequently. Those concerned with this effect might want to use stevia leaf or honey instead of licorice.

What you'll need

1 part dried goldenrod leaves and flowers (Solidago canadensis)

1 part dried lemongrass (Cymbopogon citratus)

1 part whole hawthorn berries (Crataegus spp.)

1/2 part dried ginger root (Zingiber officinale)

1/2 part dried licorice root (Glycyrrhiza glabra)

Combine all the ingredients together. (I recommend buying the above ingredients as "cut and sifted" with the exception of the hawthorn berries which work fine whole.)

To brew: Use 1 heaping tablespoon per 8 ounces of hot water. Steep covered for 5 to 15 minutes. Strain and enjoy.

Vanilla Rooibos Tea Blend

Rooibos is a delicious herbal tea that does not contain caffeine. It has a slight natural vanilla flavor that is augmented in this colorful blend.

What you'll need

2 parts rooibos tea

1 part safflower petals (Carthamus tinctorius)

1 part Calendula petals (Calendula officinalis)

1 part rose hips (Rosa spp.)

1/2 part vanilla bean, chopped finely

Combine all the ingredients together.

To brew: Use 1 heaping tablespoon per 8 ounces of hot water. Steep covered for 3 to 5 minutes. Strain and enjoy.

Making These Blends as Gifts

You can use these tea blend recipes exactly as they state, or they can be the jumping off place for you to create your own tea blends. There are endless possibilities here!

To give them as gifts, consider putting them in brown tea bags, cello bags or even corked wide-mouth bottles. Be sure to include the ingredients as well as brewing suggestions.

Mountain Rose Herbs also carries a variety of tea accessories for brewing single-cup teas that would make a nice gift along with your tea blends.

If you're battling the bulge: Try white tea

As the least processed of all the teas from the camellia sinensis plant, white tea packs the biggest polyphenol punch – as well as some promising news for dieters. In a 2009 study on human fat cells, German researchers found that white tea extract helped prevent the growth of new fat cells, while also stimulating existing fat cells to break down.

Look for a good-quality loose-leaf white tea at a specialty tea store. Loose-leaf teas tend to retain more antioxidants – and usually have more flavour – than their bagged cousins.

If you're at risk for cardiovascular disease: Try green tea

Tea does more than soothe the soul – it's good for your heart, too. While green tea is brimming with powerful disease-fighting antioxidants called catechins, one in particular – epigallocatechin gallate (EGCG) – is linked to a whole host of heart-health benefits.

According to Dr. Sandra Davidge, a professor in the department of obstetrics and gynecology at the University of Alberta in Edmonton and author of a 2008 research paper on EGCG, this catechin acts as an anti-inflammatory, protecting the cells that line the interior surface of our blood vessels. The health of these cells is crucial, she says. "If they become damaged or impaired, it can lead to high blood pressure and other vascular problems."

If you struggle with anxiety: Try chamomile tea

The results of a 2009 randomized control trial published in the Journal of Clinical Psychopharmacology suggest chamomile may be helpful in treating generalized anxiety disorder. "Chamomile is a very mild sedative," explains Evelyn Coggins, a clinical herbalist based in Pemberton, B.C. "So if you just want to calm down – but you don't want to be zonked out – a cup of chamomile tea is a great option."

Derived from the chamomile flower, the tea contains apigenin, a flavonoid and anti-anxiety agent that binds to the same receptors in the brain as prescription sedatives. Coggins recommends covering your cup or pot when steeping the tea to retain the chamomile's volatile anti-inflammatory oils, which are responsible for its calming effect and can escape in the form of steam.

If you're prone to digestive problems: Try rooibos tea

Not only is rooibos tea naturally caffeine free, it's also loaded with flavonoids – a type of polyphenol with anti-inflammatory properties. According to Dr. Nabeel Ghayur, a postdoctoral fellow at McMaster University in Hamilton who coauthored a 2006 research paper on the health benefits of rooibos, this anti-inflammatory effect can help tame tummy troubles.

"Flavonoids contribute to the relaxation of gut muscles and intestinal tissues, and can actually have an antidiarrheal effect," he says. To make the most of rooibos's stomach-soothing benefits, Ghayur recommends one to one-and-a-half teaspoons of loose-leaf rooibos steeped in 120 millilitres of water two to three times a day.

If you have hypertension: Try hibiscus tea

Blood pressure through the roof? Participants in a 2009 study from Tufts University in Massachusetts who drank three cups of hibiscus tea per day experienced a significant drop in blood pressure.

The tart red tea contains an antioxidant that scientists believe may help widen the blood vessels, allowing blood to flow more freely. You can find hibiscus in many herbal tea blends – but make sure it's listed near the top of the ingredient list, which usually indicates a higher concentration.

If you're not breathing easy: Try ginger tea

Whenever Dr. Nabeel Ghayur suffers from a respiratory ailment such as chest congestion, he reaches for a cup of ginger tea. "It tends to dilate the bronchial tree and soothe the airways," he says, noting that this effect may also help asthmatics. "Asthma patients experience constriction or narrowing of their lung airways, and anything that can relax or open up those airways tends to be of immense value." The pungent brew also contains a compound that can help suppress coughs.

If you're concerned about cancer: Try green tea

Numerous studies have garnered scientific support for green tea's anticarcinogenic effects. Not only has research linked green tea consumption with a reduced risk for breast cancer in women and advanced prostate cancer in men, but it's been shown to help prevent or slow the progress of other cancers, too.

Richard Beliveau, a professor of biochemistry at the University of Quebec in Montreal and a professor of surgery and physiology at the University of Montreal, says the brew's cancer-fighting properties boil down to its catechin content. "Catechins interfere with the growth factors associated with cancer development," he explains. "Basically, these antioxidants induce the suicide of cancer on a cellular level." Take advantage of green tea's goodness by drinking two to three 150-millilitre cups each day.

Give the health benefits of your brew an added boost with these strategies

• Steep your tea for at least five minutes. A bit of patience pays off, since the polyphenol content of your tea increases with steeping time.

• Become a dunker. Up to five times as many flavonoids (compounds with antioxidant properties) are released when you continuously dunk your tea bag or infuser.

• Add a little lemon. Tea can interfere with iron absorption, but the vitamin C in citrus can help counteract the effect.

• Reconsider decaf. Decaffeinated teas may have lower levels of beneficial flavonoids.

CONCLUSION

Blending tea is an artistic way to enjoy the unique flavour and characteristics of different ingredients in a single cup of tea. The purpose of making tea blends is to add the appealing flavour to the tea which turns the non-tea buyer to your customers.

Many herbs have medicinal properties. You can learn more about the medicinal properties of herbs by grabbing books at the library, or more commonly by reading up about them online. If you're going to go down this road, we recommend using the latin names of the herb. They look like this: Vitex agnus-castus. The common names vary much more, whereas the latin names have more consistency among herb species.

Once you know what you'd like to accomplish, you can start searching for herbs that fit the bill. You can do specific learning about some herbs here, although the information there is meant more for health practitioners.

Herbs don't always taste good, but many of them taste great. And many of them taste great when blended together. Try selecting a few of your favourite herbs and mixing them together to see what type of outcome you get.

There's something about blending herbs that is engaging. It brings us back to an older time and it gets us involved with the things we choose to consume. It's a wonderful activity to try by yourself or with a friend to see what you can come up with. It's also significantly cheaper to buy herbs in this format than it is to buy pre-packaged individual bags of tea. Save money and have fun? What's not to like.